Calling Out the People of God

*Ezekiel's Challenge
for Today's Church*

Douglas Jacoby

Calling Out the People of God
Ezekiels Challenge for Today's Church

About the author: Since 2003 Dr. Douglas Jacoby has been a freelance teacher and consultant. With degrees from Drew, Harvard, and Duke, Douglas has written 35 books, recorded over 1000 podcasts, and spoken in over 100 universities and in over 500 cities, in 126 nations around the world. For more information about the work, speaking schedule, and teaching ministry of Douglas Jacoby, visit his website at www.DouglasJacoby.com.

www.ipibooks.com

Contents

• Foreword •

In 1983 a tall American graduate student shared his faith with me in London, England. I did not believe in God but I was curious. He answered my questions patiently, baptized me, baptized my future husband, and three years later performed our wedding ceremony (in three different languages!). Through the years, my friendship with Douglas Jacoby has withstood the storms of life and ministry. Wherever we have moved in the world, we have stayed connected, and I have the utmost respect for him, Vicki, and his family.

This book on Ezekiel is very challenging, especially for those of us in leadership. As challenging and thought-provoking as it is, however, Douglas's book is not as hardline as the book of Ezekiel itself. Throughout the Bible, God reserves his strongest expectations—and judgment—for leaders. God holds leaders to a higher standard (James 3:1). Leadership is a high calling and an incredible responsibility. No one is perfect, of course. It is crucial, however, that we not be hypocrites, and that we hold ourselves to the standards we expect of others. We are called to imitate Jesus, and that includes not just his deeds or his evangelism, but also his character.

At the beginning of the book, Douglas refers to a clarion call. Ezekiel raised the alarm. Israel was not in a good place. This same clarion call is needed today. The church is supposed to imitate the heart of Jesus, and "leaders are to feed, strengthen, and heal." Sadly, too often the modern-day church—especially in the minority world (formerly known as the first world)—is more focused on dogma and drawing lines in the sand than on being a safe and nurturing place. The church can become a place of trauma and abuse rather than a shelter from the storms of the world as God intends. As a French person living in Nepal, I can testify that the church in other parts of the world is much closer to the church we read about in the Bible. In many countries I have visited, be it in Africa, South or East Asia, etc., people value community and look out for one another in a way that is, sadly, quite foreign to the wealthier Western world.

Having been in leadership for pretty much my whole Christian life, I have fallen into many of the traps this book describes. I certainly gave in to the corporate model of church growth, watching numbers and keeping statistics. Douglas raises the question, How do we evaluate our ministries—by numbers or by our "faithfulness to an uncompromised mission"? The pursuit of "ministry success" can lead us to overlook the needs of the people in our congregations. We can resort to bullying tactics and insensitive methods of getting short-term results. We can have unrealistic expectations and exacting standards that leave very little space for grace and compassion. I have certainly done all of the above under the disguise of "faith" and "vision," and for that I am really sorry.

Another trap we can fall into is the trap of selecting certain sins to harp on. We can preach at length about not being like "the world," modesty, purity, lack of commitment (is that a sin?), social media use (again, is that a sin?), rebellion, and divisiveness. We rarely hear sermons on materialism (a sin that is plaguing the Western church), apathy toward the poor, arrogance, fits of rage, or slander. How many times as a leader have I policed the clothes a young lady was wearing, while at home I would lose my temper with my children? There is much danger in picking which sins are more acceptable than others.

Douglas also brings up the question of how much of the church finances goes to help the poor and how much goes to salaries and buildings. Should we pay the salaries of our ministers? Absolutely. Should we pay for buildings? Maybe. Should we help the poor and the marginalized? Without question (Ezekiel 16:49). Should that be a bigger priority? Definitely. I witness daily the physical needs of our brothers, sisters, and neighbors. The mother of one of our students at the HOPE *worldwide* school in Kathmandu is so poor that she did not eat for two weeks, and she told no one. When we found out, we of course helped her, but this kind of situation is not unusual.

As many of us are getting older, Douglas urges us to keep "the suppleness of a youthful and obedient heart." However old and experienced we are, we need to maintain a learning spirit. He talks about not just making adjustments, but rather, looking at things with fresh eyes. We need to be willing to repent and take a hard stance when it comes to following Jesus. The youth in our churches are questioning us, and rightly so. And so the clarion comes. Much is going on in the world right now. COVID-19 has taken many loved ones away before their time. It has separated us from each other and locked us in our homes and in front of our screens. This great global tragedy could also be used by God for good (Romans 8:28). Could the COVID-19 crisis be part of the sound of the clarion, an appeal by God for us to reassess our priorities? Do we hear its resounding call?

Nadine Templer
Kathmandu, Nepal

• Preface •

This book is a compilation of the 2019 Ezekiel series that appears in ten installments in my newsletters[1] and at my website. Most of the concerns are as relevant in our times as they were in the days of the prophet, regardless of where we go to church or in what nation we live. After all, the Old Testament Scriptures have much to teach us—and they are practical:

> But as for you [Timothy], continue in what you have learned and have become convinced of, because you know those from whom you learned it, and how from infancy you have known the Holy Scriptures, which are able to make you wise for salvation through faith in Christ Jesus. All Scripture is God-breathed and is useful for teaching, rebuking, correcting and training in righteousness, so that the servant of God may be thoroughly equipped for every good work (2 Timothy 3:14–17).

> For everything that was written in the past was written to teach us, so that through the endurance taught in the Scriptures and the encouragement they provide we might have hope (Romans 15:4; see also 1 Corinthians 10:11).

The series received an overwhelmingly positive response from all continents, age groups, and varieties of ministry. You can read a sampling of the responses in the appendix to this little book. The degree of support I have felt from brothers and sisters all around the world has been both uplifting and fortifying. Yet if the number of newsletter subscription cancellations is an indication, it seems not everyone felt the same. But please know that this series—with the issues it revealed—was emotionally challenging for my wife and me. As we fasted and prayed for clarity, we felt great pressure, slept less, and were humbled by what God was showing us.

I hope no one thinks I feel above receiving the challenging message myself. I love the church, and I ache for her to be the pure bride for which Christ longs (Ephesians 5:23; Revelation 21:2). But it's not enough for me or you only to talk about our vision. We must live it—all of us, regardless of our spiritual age or ministry in the church.

• Overview •

1. Clarion Call

It is the sixth century BC, and all is not well among God's people. Ezekiel is chosen to warn Judah about their perilous spiritual condition. Whether or not they respond, he is to declare Yahweh's word.

2. False Optimism

The leaders of God's people naively (or perhaps stubbornly) ignore the warning signs, assuming *their* group is unique—and favored by God.

3. Shallow Repentance

Judah's impending disaster is dramatized, just as multiple illustrations are available to enable us to visualize spiritual reality—and take to heart God's word.

4. Yahweh Calls Out the Shepherds—and the Sheep:

The leaders are failing to feed the flock, deal with sin, and model humility. The sheep are hardly innocent, either.

5. Ezekiel Reprimands the False Prophets

The establishment prophets whitewash sin. Even today, tolerant, "mature" preachers and company men whitewash the sins of God's people.

6. Ingratitude and Infidelity

Spiritual thanklessness and adultery characterize the people of sixth-century Judah—and most "Christians" in our own day.

7. The Lord Is Just

Yahweh's standards are righteous, yet his call to holiness is routinely ignored. He is not unjust, nor does he desire that any perish.

8. Stand in the Gap!

Rather than standing around waiting for God's people to repent or for leaders to lead the way, let's courageously take the initiative.

9. A Beautiful Singer?

Even though the prophet's credibility was high, his words manifestly on target, too many of God's people prefer entertainment over challenge.

10. Glorious Future

Yahweh's will is that we live holy lives in his glorious presence. Yet, like ancient Judah, the church today lacks the willpower to live holy and obedient lives.

1   • Clarion Call •

hat exactly is a clarion call? Clarion means "clear and shrill." A clarion call has been defined as "a strongly expressed demand or request for action" (*Oxford English Dictionary*). The call comes to the 30-year-old priest Ezekiel, in exile in Babylon, by one of the irrigation canals crisscrossing the land of Mesopotamia. There is actually a *double* clarion call in the early chapters of Ezekiel. Yahweh calls the prophet Ezekiel—the first call—entrusting him to sound the call to faithless Israel—the second call.

> *In my thirtieth year, in the fourth month on the fifth day, while I was among the exiles by the Kebar River, the heavens were opened and I saw visions of God. On the fifth of the month—it was the fifth year of the exile of King Jehoiachin—the word of the LORD came to Ezekiel the priest, the son of Buzi, by the Kebar River in the land of the Babylonians. There the hand of the LORD was on him (1:1–3).*

Thus, the call to God's people to repent—and above all to their leaders—flows from the call of Ezekiel to prophetic ministry. The prophet is deeply disturbed by the message. Like the eighth-century BC Isaiah and Ezekiel's sixth-century contemporary Jeremiah, he initially resists the call (Isaiah 6; Jeremiah 1). Ezekiel is overwhelmed. Faced with the daunting task of confronting fellow prophets and leaders, as well as his own countrymen, he is fearful (2:6; see Joshua 1:9; Jeremiah 1:6–8)—even angry and bitter (3:14–15). The prophet requires serious nudging. Ever been that way? I suppose all of us have. It can be easier to speak frankly to a complete unbeliever than to those who sit in the pew with us. It's the fifth year of the exile of king Jehoiachin, or 592 BC.

> *He said to me, "Son of man, stand up on your feet and I will speak to you." As he spoke, the Spirit came into me and raised me to my feet, and I heard him speaking to me. He said: "Son of man, I am sending you to the Israelites, to a rebellious nation that has rebelled against me; they and their ancestors have been in revolt against me to this very day" (2:1–3).*

The Boom Comes Down

Why the urgent clarion call? Yahweh's people are required to be faithful to the covenant. Their salvation—like ours—is *dependent* on remaining in a relationship with God. Disobedience, Yahweh had warned, would lead to increasingly severe measures, the ultimate of which was exile—removal from the Promised Land (Deuteronomy 28; Leviticus 26). Such a punishment had already been meted out to eighth-century-BC Israel (the northern kingdom). The Assyrians dragged the unfaithful tribes into exile (2 Kings 17), having destroyed their capital city of Samaria in 722 BC. Most of the southern kingdom of Judah had also succumbed to the armies of Assyria, yet Jerusalem—thanks to the faith of King Hezekiah—was spared (701 BC). Judah, for the moment, was secure.

Babylon defeated Assyria in the early seventh century BC, taking captives from Judah in 605 and 597. It was in 597 that Ezekiel was led to Babylon, along with 10,000 other Judeans.

The (true) prophets warn that Judah will not be spared if she doesn't give up her idolatry and turn in repentance to her God. Yet many Judeans refuse to believe that the holy city can fall. They imagine that Yahweh's prophets, like Jeremiah—and soon Ezekiel—are overreacting and exaggerating the failures of the leaders and the nation. Yet the boom *will* come down. In 586 BC Jerusalem will fall—just as it will fall again nearly seven centuries later (once the city and temple have been rebuilt) to the Roman armies, in AD 70.

Dislocation and Disappointment

The entire nation has been dislocated, the northern kingdom in the eighth century, and the southern kingdom in three waves of attack and deportation around the turn of the sixth century. Removed from their land, Israel experiences a crisis of faith and a deep longing for their homeland (Psalm 126; 137). For the priest Ezekiel, it must have been deeply disappointing, as he was now 30 years old—the age at which he would have commenced priestly duties in the Jerusalem temple (Numbers 4:3). Yet he is in nowhere near Jerusalem, but in exile in Babylon. Will he ever see Jerusalem again?

> *"The people to whom I am sending you are obstinate and stubborn. Say to them, 'This is what the Sovereign LORD says.' And whether they listen or fail to listen—for they are a rebellious people—they will know that a prophet has been among them. And you, son of man, do not be afraid of them or their words. Do not be afraid, though briers and thorns are all around you and you live among scorpions. Do not be afraid of what they say or be terrified by them, though they are a rebellious people. You must speak my words to them, whether they listen or fail to listen, for they are rebellious. But you, son of man, listen to what I say to you. Do not rebel like that rebellious people"* (2:4–8).

Declaring the Truth

Ezekiel has a message to declare. If he refuses to speak, he will be little different from his compatriots: rebellious. For Ezekiel, a successful prophetic ministry does not require that the exiles repent, only that *he* faithfully deliver the message. How often we evaluate ministry by the number who respond, instead of by our faithfulness to an uncompromised mission. This is a mistake.

> *And he said to me, "Son of man, eat what is before you, eat this scroll; then go and speak to the people of Israel." So I opened my mouth, and he gave me the scroll to eat. Then he said to me, "Son of man, eat*

this scroll I am giving you and fill your stomach with it." So I ate it, and it tasted as sweet as honey in my mouth (3:1–3).

Like Jeremiah (Jeremiah 15:16) and John (Revelation 10:9–10), he must eat the scroll—"words of lament and mourning and woe" (3:10)—so thoroughly digesting the bittersweet message that it becomes a part of him. Ezekiel's mission is also like that of a watchman.

At the end of seven days the word of the LORD came to me: "Son of man, I have made you a watchman for the people of Israel; so hear the word I speak and give them warning from me. When I say to a wicked person, 'You will surely die,' and you do not warn them or speak out to dissuade them from their evil ways in order to save their life, that wicked person will die for their sin, and I will hold you accountable for their blood. But if you do warn the wicked person and they do not turn from their wickedness or from their evil ways, they will die for their sin; but you will have saved yourself" (3:16–19).

The Lord is reasonable. He honors genuine repentance, as surely as he punishes disobedience. (For more on the reasonableness of God's expectation of obedience, see Ezekiel 18:1–32, a passage that helped me enormously as a new believer.) Ezekiel is to be God's channel for the summons to repentance. He is God's designated "watchman." It is fair to ask, Are we all watchmen?

- There is a sense in which we are called to be our brother's keeper (Genesis 4:9; 1 Thessalonians 5:14-15).

- As for evangelism, it is the mission and lifeblood of the church (Matthew 28:18–20).

- Yet God's words to Ezekiel are not equally God's word to us; not all are called to be prophets.

- We may not all be watchmen in the same way, yet those who know Christ cannot but speak out. "We cannot stop speaking about what we have seen and heard" (Acts 4:20), and "If I say, 'I will not remember him or speak anymore in His name,' then in my heart it becomes like a burning fire shut up in my bones; and I am weary of holding it in, and I cannot endure it" (Jeremiah 20:9). We are accountable to God for what we do with our knowledge (Hebrews 4:13).

- Yet it is the special duty of church leaders—and above all, those with the title of evangelist—to lead the way. Biblically it seems an evangelist is a church planter, someone willing to preach where Christ is unknown—even if it's risky. The evangelist is not an administrator—a comfortable "senior pastor" as in many churches in our time. Yet many evangelists are ministry administrators far more than they are the church's interface with a lost world.

Reflection:

Decisions:

2 • False Optimism •

In this chapter, I will articulate observations and thoughts I've been contemplating during many years of travel across the United States and the globe.

As Balanced as a Firebrand

When I posted the series in my newsletter, "Ezekiel: Clarion Call" was a strong lesson—but that's the nature of the prophets. I have found Ezekiel to be challenging to me too, and it would have been more comfortable *not* to relay the message. Yet many of you have asked me not to hold back—you want to be called higher. When one grateful reader asked whether the first article was balanced, I responded that it was "as balanced as a firebrand can be." (At this I smiled.)

The following critiques *all* forms of Christianity. These words apply directly to the family of churches among which I most often fellowship. I write them not in bitterness, but in hope that they may strike a chord—with impact.

Dire Straits

Like Judah of old, the church of our time is in serious trouble. Like Israel, we have allowed idols to displace wholehearted devotion to Yahweh. We bow down to idols of comfort, wealth, and financial security; fashion and popularity; political and military power; sex and pleasure;

sports, recreation, and entertainment. The pursuit of *holiness*—without which no one will see the Lord (Hebrews 12:14)—has been exchanged for a cheap and shallow pursuit of *happiness*.

In our day, most churches are in a state of rebellion—although it's often called "maturity." ("Let's not get too excited, or we may drive people away from Christ or, even worse, being accused of being radical or cultic.") Our disobedience is dressed up in the guise of "tolerance" or defended in the lingo of freedom in Christ, and we justify our mediocrity by claiming to be purely grace-motivated.

As I scan the landscape of contemporary Christianity—including most of the churches where I speak and fellowship—I can't help but see the parallels with ancient Israel. The nonchalance, inertia, and spiritual lethargy are increasingly visible and defended. Resistance to biblical instruction is the norm. Fewer and fewer disciples submit to the daily discipline of prayer and study, or to a lifestyle of submission, self-denial, and sacrificial living. Church has become all about making people happy: being attractively acceptable to outsiders and not too challenging for insiders. Worship services cater to seeker comfort and perky music. There is more energy from musical amplification than from hearts on fire for God. The sermons are shorter, with fewer calls for repentance and genuine expectations for people to actually obey. We've exchanged living the answers for knowing the answers. The great victories of faith seem to be in the past, and we now live vicariously through some new convert in the teen ministry. Discipleship is optional, and so are most events outside of Sunday morning.

The lack of growth—spiritual and numerical—is deeply concerning. Leadership aims to "hold our own," "be stable" or at least not to shrink. Faithfulness once described a well-rounded life of seeking first the Kingdom. Now it fits anyone who at least attends on Sunday morning and gives a financial contribution. It's become obvious that many churches are in a state of contraction. Moreover, we are blending in with the surrounding religious culture. What is distinctive—how are we any different? Churchgoing Protestants come on Sundays, but not necessarily to small group meetings or church classes. In a recent survey of US churches, for example, it was discovered that 38% come on Sunday only, 28% come to further meetings one to three times a month, and 35% to four or more meetings a month.[2] This matches very closely the pattern I have seen in my own fellowship.

Are our hearts touched by heaven's fire, or are we a people without a message? (Let's answer these questions honestly.) From my viewpoint—and my perspective as one who has visited hundreds of churches—we are in dire straits. Our lampstand may soon be removed (Revelation 2:5)—if it hasn't already been taken away. So why such resistance to the message?

False Hope

Again, the parallels with ancient Israel are instructive. Their leaders and the people resisted the prophetic message because of unbridled optimism. To them, it was simply unthinkable that Yahweh could abandon his people. After all, he had given them an eternal covenant. He had gifted them with the land of Canaan, a permanent possession. The Davidic kingship was another promise, as was Zion—where Yahweh met with his people in the holy temple. (See 2 Samuel 7:13; Deuteronomy 1:8; etc.; and esp. Psalm 89.)

These four blessings were irrevocable—in their misguided thinking. Yet they had forgotten that all these promises and covenants were *conditional* (Exodus 19:5; Leviticus 26:44; Joshua 23:16; etc.). What tapes (or podcasts) are playing in our minds? What do we tell ourselves that prevents us from waking up (Revelation 3:2)? Four things come to mind:

- **"We are unique; no one else teaches a message of radical discipleship."** We may tell ourselves this, but it's manifestly untrue. Many groups are serious about discipleship, holiness, and radical Christian living. I meet leaders of such groups fairly often, and many of them lead lives that are an upward call to me—as they are to many of my readers.

We purchase books on church growth written by leaders from across a broad spectrum of churches. Besides, what we may have taught and believed 20 or 30 years ago does not justify us *now*, if we're not walking the walk. See Ezekiel 18! True discipleship is walking as Jesus walked, not one-over-one discipling, or plugging into various church programs (meetings, fundraisers, conferences, and so on).

- **"We hold the correct teaching on conversion."** We know that no one is "born" a Christian. There is no salvation without the second birth—without faith, repentance, and baptism (John 3:16; 3:21; 3:5). We find it unthinkable that God would pass us over in favor of those whose theology lacks crispness and correctness. Yet there are multiple groups, not just one, who still retain the original apostolic teaching. ("Christians only, but not the only Christians.") Further, we forget that God has often exalted the outsider, while the insider forfeited his blessings (see Romans 2:26). The Lord looks at the heart, as well as the fruit of our lives (1 Samuel 16:7; Matthew 7:20).

- **"Our numerical growth shows that we are [or were] on the right path."** But hasn't the Lord warned us of the danger of relying on numbers (2

Samuel 24:1–17)? Does the New Testament showcase the growth statistics of the churches? Hardly. Apart from the count of the men baptized in Acts 2:41 and 4:4, along with the vague "myriads" (Greek) of Acts 21:20, no numbers are given at all. And even then, the figures are only approximate. (For more on this, please see my 2000 paper "Statistics and Church Growth."[3]) So, *are* we growing? Where are most of our new converts after five years? Ten years? A fully honest look at statistics must be longitudinal, not a mere annual report—let alone one that highlights impressive figures without analyzing them against the backdrop of previous years, grounding new converts in the Word, plans for ongoing discipling, and so forth.

- **"The blood of Jesus cleanses us from sin, so even if our obedience falls short, that's okay."** But 1 John 1:7 doesn't guarantee forgiveness if we don't "walk in the light." The grace of God never promises to cover willful disobedience to his word. No one will live in perfect submission, but the Lord does expect that we sincerely follow Christ, walking as he did (1 John 2:3–6).

In short, we tell ourselves many things that merely excuse our lack of obedience—or so we think. For these reasons—and I realize there are more—we too easily dismiss calls to discipleship as immature, unnecessary, or simplistic. We have much more in common with the people of Ezekiel's day.

God's Presence

Despite the hard words above (mine), and the severe message given to Ezekiel for his people, there was hope. The glory (presence) of God—moving in his heavenly chariot, the cherubim—accompanied the exiles to Babylon. While the Lord had abandoned his holy city and temple, he had not completely forsaken the exiles. (Not all were ungodly, even if the majority were.) Further, when in the staggering vision of Ezekiel 1 the prophet beholds the throne, it is not the king of Babylon who sits upon it, but Yahweh, the Lord Almighty (1:26 etc.). There is hope. Despite the fiery preaching of the first 24 chapters, in which Ezekiel aims to convince his countrymen of the coming judgment, encouraging words and visions of the future will appear later in the book.

Reflection:

Decisions:

Reflection:

3 • Shallow Repentance •

For 24 chapters, Ezekiel pleads with the people of God to take the prophetic warning seriously. Yet their hearts weren't sensitive; there was little repentance. Let me share with you one of my wife's insights: As young Christians we resembled Zacchaeus more than the Rich Young Ruler (Matthew 19; Mark 10; Luke 18). But now we're the Rich *Old* Ruler (or as a friend recently told me, "We've become our fathers."). Financial prosperity, time for relaxation and repose, and grumpy excuses that often come with age have eroded the suppleness of a youthful and obedient heart. Notice that Zacchaeus calls Jesus "Lord" (Luke 19:8), whereas the rich guy only calls him "good teacher" (Luke 18:18). Are these lessons from Ezekiel only "good teaching," or do they serve as a clarion call to follow Jesus as Lord? (See Ezekiel 33:30–33.)

There had been glimmers of hope. The revival under Josiah (621 BC) was one of the bright moments of Old Testament history. Yet complacency quickly overshadowed Josiah's good intentions; since his death *all* the kings of Judah were bad. The Assyrians had conquered the northern kingdom of Israel (which fell in 722); the Babylonians had twice come for the southern kingdom of Judah (605 and 507). The writing was on the wall. In fact, in a few short years everything the Judaeans cherished would be destroyed.

Making the Warning Concrete

Like us, the people of old appreciated the truth more clearly through visual aids. When the truth is portrayed in parable, in an illustration, or through drama, the abstract becomes concrete. Hardness of heart makes us deaf to the Bible. As a result, prophetic warnings are no longer enough; dramatization must lend power to the message. It enables us to visualize divine truths we can no longer hear.

The book of Ezekiel is full of visual aids, of which we will mention three.

Jerusalem: "Model" City

The coming disaster is portrayed by means of a replica of Jerusalem:

> *"And you, son of man, take a brick and set it in front of you. Inscribe a city on it—Jerusalem. Lay siege to it! Build siege works against it. Erect a siege ramp against it! Post soldiers outside it and station battering rams around it. Then take an iron pan, place it as an iron wall between you and the city and turn your face toward it. It will be under siege, and you shall besiege it. This will be a sign to the people of Israel.*
>
> *"Then lie on your left side and put the sin of the people of Israel upon yourself. You are to bear their sin for the number of days you lie on your side. I have assigned you the same number of days as the years of their sin. So for 390 days you will bear the sin of the people of Israel"* (4:1–5 NET).

Imagine if Ezekiel had fashioned a model of our church building—which *should* be a powerful vector of the gospel message. Yet does our lifestyle convey this message? Please read the whole of chapter 4—and keep going. You will find numerous vivid enactments and graphic illustrations you might not even read in mixed company. The Lord was trying to shock the sensibilities of his people so they would have every opportunity to grasp the truth—and to respond.

Escaping through the Wall

In chapter 12, Ezekiel takes on the persona of a refugee, digging through a wall (representing Jerusalem's city wall). In a few short years, the Judaeans would be trying by all possible means to escape divine judgment at the hands of the Babylonians.

> "Therefore, son of man, pack up your belongings as if for exile. During the day, while they are watching, pretend to go into exile. Go from where you live to another place. Perhaps they will understand, although they are a rebellious house. Bring out your belongings packed for exile during the day while they are watching. And go out at evening, while they are watching, as if for exile. While they are watching, dig a hole in the wall and carry your belongings out through it. While they are watching, raise your baggage onto your shoulder and carry it out in the dark. You must cover your face so that you cannot see the ground because I have made you an object lesson to the house of Israel" (12:3–6 NET).

The Shock of Unspeakable Tragedy

The reality of the situation tends not to be clear without the visual component. In chapter 24, Yahweh instructs Ezekiel to mourn the death of his wife quietly—without the customary wailing, funeral singers, and other traditions. This was a truly bitter pill to swallow. Imagine the pain. (For anyone who has lost a spouse or your closest friend, this should not be too hard to do.)

> *"Son of man, realize that I am about to take the delight of your eyes away from you with a jolt, but you must not mourn or weep or shed tears. Groan in silence for the dead, but do not perform mourning rites. Bind on your turban and put your sandals on your feet. Do not cover your lip and do not eat food brought by others." So I spoke to the people in the morning, and my wife died in the evening. In the morning I acted just as I was commanded. Then the people said to me, "Will you not tell us what these things you are doing mean for us?" (24:16–19 NET)*

Ezekiel's emotional self-control is astounding. Everyone would have understood his demeanor if he had ignored the Lord's command. Yet he obeyed, and became a walking illustration of the profound sadness of Judah's true state.

More Where These Came From

These are just three out of the dozens of illustrations and visual aids in the 48 chapters of Ezekiel. Judah was without excuse when the third wave of Babylonians besieged Jerusalem in 586 BC, leveling the Holy City and Solomon's Temple (nearly four centuries old—built in 956 BC).

Dramatic Illustrations for the Church

As we have seen, through Ezekiel's ministry the Lord provided abundant illustrations of the judgment to come. Without these visualizations, even those with tender hearts toward God's word may not have repented. We all benefit from illustrations. Here are four places where we can discern the real condition of many churches today:

- **Buildings, bulletins, and websites.** Most Bible-centered churches follow the evangelical model—quite similar to the American business model. The "CEO" (senior pastor) and his officers (like staff members, elders, small group leaders, satellite leaders) monitor the bottom line: attendance, conversions, and contributions. It easily becomes all about a vision for growth, allegiance to the plan, and efforts to fulfill the CEO's vision—"dramatically" illustrated in bottom-line statistics. Yet when we honestly look at the bottom line, it is clear that (1) few churches are growing, (2) those that are growing frequently rely on faulty theology or leadership, or else most of their growth consists of transfers from other churches, and (3) since children are usually counted in total attendance, the figures are skewed—suggesting that more members are showing up on Sunday than is the case. We have glossy church bulletins, attractive buildings, or hotel meeting venues in the best parts of town. We spend tens of thousands of dollars on church websites that communicate a dynamism that is far from the reality. Do these reflect the true condition of the church? This is not to denigrate good work being done by godly leaders around the globe. Of course, some churches are healthy. But they appear to be in the minority.

- **Church history.** Scouring the record of 20 centuries, we notice patterns, with multiple lessons to be learned. Do we lack the humility to learn from the past? Throughout history—in every century—there were groups who considered themselves to be God's *only* faithful remnant. Of course, it's easier to claim, "Those other groups weren't real Christians—so we can safely ignore them." Yet we ignore them at our peril. Wise church leaders learn from the past. They are students of church history.

- **Old Testament history.** Then there is the "church" (assembly) of Old Testament times. The history of God's people in OT times is replete with warnings and lessons for us (1 Corinthians 10:11; Romans 15:4; 2 Peter 3:1–2; 2 Timothy 3:16–17). When I was a young Christian, I was puzzled as to why so rarely were the people of Israel wholeheartedly following Yahweh. Now it makes more sense. Like the 2000 years of church history, Old Testament history, which spans more than 1000 years, gives us multiple vital visuals. Do we really think we can ignore the first three-quarters of Scripture? Ask yourself: Do I read, or only listen to podcasts? Do I have biblical convictions, or are my opinions determined by the ideas of the teachers who most appeal to my interest? Biblical knowledge among most congregations is at an all-time low. Most churches provide few opportunities for in-depth teaching. And when they do, participation is optional. New converts are not grounded in the foundations of the faith. Scripture memorization is considered too much to ask.

- **Church visits.** Finally, even if we were new to the faith (knowing little of biblical history), or new to leadership (perhaps ignorant of church history), or lacked access to spreadsheets and church bulletins, we could visit Bible-centered churches—those who are commmited to following God's word—and open our eyes. That doesn't mean that we agree with every doctrine they teach. But we humbly learn from the good things they're doing. This provides a powerful visual indeed! My own observations from speaking in various denominations worldwide (though mainly in churches in the Restoration Movement) strongly support this viewpoint: Ezekiel's clarion call is desperately needed.

Could the severity of the situation be any clearer? Then as now, multiple illustrations are available to enable us to visualize spiritual reality and appreciate the relevance and power of God's word (Hebrews 4:12). Thank you, Ezekiel.

Reflection:

Decisions:

Reflection:

4   Yahweh Calls Out • the Shepherds • —and the Sheep

Spiritual (or unspiritual) leadership is a pervasive theme in the book of Ezekiel. In this book, and in this chapter in particular, I do *not* mean to imply that all church leadership has failed. Many leaders may feel burdened and weary—I can relate. It is not through malice or a bad heart that they are seeing diminishing returns on their work and unresponsive listeners to their message. There are certainly godly men and women serving congregations worldwide, just as there are healthy churches. Yet most are *not* healthy. As in Ezekiel's day, compromise with the world is far and away the norm. Further, as church leaders we tend to let down the members in similar ways. There are numerous parallels between Ezekiel's day and our own.

Note: While "shepherds" in the New Testament refers to elders—the primary overseers of the church, evidenced by the high standard of character and conduct to which they are called (1 Timothy 3:1-7; Titus 1:5-9)[4]—the principles in this article apply to all leaders. (And, as we shall soon see, all God's people, whether leaders or not.)

Reptile Worship and Sun Worship
    In chapter 8:13–17, Ezekiel (in a vision) is shown

idolatrous images being worshipped by Israel's leaders: "Do you see, son of man, what the elders of the house of Israel are doing in the dark, each in the chamber of his idolatrous images? For they think, 'The Lord does not see us!'" (8:12).

Idols (images) of crawling things and unclean animals (8:10) were common in the region in Ezekiel's time. For example, Egypt, Babylon, and Canaan worshipped serpent deities. While Israel's elders were outwardly respectable, truth be told they were not so different from the elders of the pagans. Their loyalties were divided between the world (with its various forms of idolatry) and Yahweh (who demands exclusive covenant loyalty). Yet the Lord sees the heart—just as easily as he sees every image we view.

Modern Idols

What "images" do we secretly venerate? Are we enslaved to online sin, whether social media, porn, gambling, gaming (fantasy sports), or shopping? A recent poll of 1351 ministers revealed that over 50 percent had viewed pornography during the recent year.[5] Whether church leaders themselves struggle with these things or not, a secret private life affects the entire body of Christ. Godly leaders not only hate sin, but also keep the flock accountable. But few leaders today are willing to tackle the epidemic of pornography or runaway screen time, or they feel powerless to address it. In many cases, it seems likely, this is because they themselves are caught up in the same web of addiction.

> *He then brought me into the inner court of the house of the LORD, and there at the entrance to the temple, between the portico and the altar, were about twenty-five men. With their backs toward the temple of the LORD and their faces toward the east, they were bowing down to the sun in the east* (8:16).

These 25 sun-worshippers were *elders* of God's people (9:6). Sometimes as we age we no longer see (or hear) as well as we once did—physically and spiritually! They had turned their backs to the Holy Place, their faces toward the rising sun. The temple was so located that worshippers would be facing west, with their backs to the morning sun. (Do the 25 men represent the 24 orders of priests—see 1 Chronicles 24:7–13—plus the high priest himself?) So, in addition to the serpent deities, Israel's leaders worshipped the sun—like nearly every culture in the ancient world. And that's the point: Israel's leaders had bought into the values of the world.

Doubtless the sun *felt* more powerful—more real—than Yahweh. After all, the sun was what drove agriculture. It was enormously easier to put one's faith in nature, kings (1 Samuel 8:5–22), armies (Psalm 20:7), or silver and gold (Deuteronomy 7:25; 17:17).

We may not worship the sun, but—especially as we

grow older—we place excessive stock in economics, security, investments, home ownership... idolatry is a danger.

We worship what is most important to us. In the world, sex, drugs, power, leisure, sports, and money are common gods. It's easier to put our faith in science, politics, or the retirement fund than to trust in Yahweh. Technology is more real to us than the power of God. It provides instant gratification, a window on the world, and opportunities for quick advancement in our career. Why invest time with God when I can quickly have thousands of "friends"? The temptation to put our faith in the things of the world is as powerful today as it was in the sixth century BC.

Marked for Destruction

In Ezekiel 9 the righteous were marked for protection—the opposite of the function of the mark in Revelation 13:16 (for destruction). Those not marked would be struck down, and it was time for judgment to begin with the leaders (9:6).

> "Go through the city of Jerusalem and put a mark on the foreheads of the people who moan and groan over all the abominations practiced in it." While I listened, he said to the others, "Go through the city after him and strike people down; do not let your eye pity nor spare anyone! Old men, young men, young women, little children, and women—wipe them out! But do not touch anyone who has the mark. Begin at my sanctuary!" So they began with the elders who were at the front of the temple (9:4–6 NET).

Shepherds and Sheep

Sin has consequences. All sin will be judged, and yet those with power, influence, leadership, resources, or a voice are especially accountable (James 3:1).

The word of the LORD came to me: "Son of man, prophesy against the shepherds of Israel; prophesy, and say to them—to the shepherds: 'This is what the sovereign LORD says: Woe to the shepherds of Israel who have been feeding themselves! Should not shepherds feed the flock? You eat the fat, you clothe yourselves with the wool, you slaughter the choice animals, but you do not feed the sheep!'" (34:1–3 NET)

The challenge applied to kings, elders, priests—the entire leadership system. Godly leaders in our day must feed the flock—take care of their needs. This includes spiritual feeding—teaching them the word of God, an area of weakness in most congregations.

"You have not strengthened the weak, healed the sick, bandaged the injured, brought back the strays, or sought the lost, but with force and harshness you have ruled over them. They were scattered because they had no shepherd, and they became food for every wild beast. My sheep wandered over all the mountains and on every high hill. My sheep were scattered over the entire face of the earth with no one looking or searching for them" (34:4–6 NET).

Leaders are to feed, strengthen, and heal. Shepherds are to bring the sheep to safe pasture for food and water.

Not being transformed by the Word, or perhaps failing to continue to learn it, leaders have not been able to present the Scriptures with depth, conviction, and impact. This too has caused the sheep to scatter. Leaders are also charged with bringing back the strays—those who have wandered off through their own fault, as well as those who have been driven off through harsh or indifferent leadership. Sometimes leaders succumb to the temptation to misuse power (Matthew 4:8–9; 20:25–28), lording it over others, all the while not practicing what they preach.

> *"For this is what the sovereign LORD says: Look, I myself will search for my sheep and seek them out. As a shepherd seeks out his flock when he is among his scattered sheep, so I will seek out my flock... I myself will feed my sheep and I myself will make them lie down, declares the sovereign LORD. I will seek the lost and bring back the strays; I will bandage the injured and strengthen the sick, but the fat and the strong I will destroy. I will feed them—with judgment!"* (34:11–12, 15–16 NET).

Yet it is not only leadership with which the Lord is displeased. The people have also failed to obey God's voice. Many churchgoers simply have no stomach for strong preaching. (More on that when we get to chapter 33.) This is a critical breakdown of both leadership and followership. The sheep have not taken advantage of opportunities to be fed—which in turn has not made leadership rewarding and enjoyable (Hebrews 13:17).

> "As for you, my sheep, this is what the sovereign LORD says: Look, I am about to judge between one sheep and another, between rams and goats. Is it not enough for you to feed on the good pasture, that you must trample the rest of your pastures with your feet? When you drink clean water, must you muddy the rest of the water by trampling it with your feet?"... "Therefore, this is what the sovereign LORD says to them: Look, I myself will judge between the fat sheep and the lean sheep... I will judge between one sheep and another." (34:17–18, 20, 22 NET).

Willing Sheep?

This year my wife and I joined a small group in our neighborhood. We share about our outreach, failings, and goals, and we report back—there's accountability. This is good for us! It's been refreshing *and* challenging. Of course, no one can make you join such a group or be open. Human sheep (unlike ovines, who often must be coerced), have to be willing. Are *we* willing? When was the last time we actually shared our *faith* (not just inviting someone to a Christian meeting)? When was the last time we *voluntarily* confessed sin? How about spending *time* (and perhaps money) for the needy? When was the last time that church felt like family? Shepherds and sheep alike need to be willing—and invested.

> "I will set one shepherd over them, and he will feed them——namely, my servant David. He will feed them and will be their shepherd. I, the LORD, will be their God, and my servant David will be prince among them; I, the LORD, have spoken!" (34:23–24 NET)

If the elders of Israel won't do their duty, Yahweh will intervene. One day he will come personally to shepherd his people. A Davidic king will rule them (10:23–24). Since David died c. 970 BC, this is not a reincarnation of David—any more than John the Baptist was a reincarnation of Elijah (Malachi 4:5; Matthew 11:14; John 1:21). Christians, who follow the Good Shepherd, know that this prophecy was fulfilled in the ministry of Jesus Christ, the Son of David (John 10:11–18; Hebrews 13:20).

No One Unscathed

Shepherds and sheep alike are called to repentance. No one is unscathed. One of our readers responded:

> Is the deeper problem with the leaders or the members? I'd say *both*. Leaders may be afraid of members' reactions (baggage from the past). Yet many members are willing to be challenged and to change. The root issue may be love growing cold (Revelation 2:4). I would think with a strong love for God we could all be on the same page—and trying to save souls.

The Takeaway

What needs to change in order for us to be a pure church pleasing to God? Here are a few things. (I realize this list is too short.)

1. Shepherds are to feed the flock (Jude 12).
We do not live on bread alone, but on every word that comes from the mouth of God (Deuteronomy

8:3). Most find little biblical depth in their local congregations—and either languish or are forced to turn elsewhere. "The ministry of the Word" (Acts 6:4) includes teaching the full counsel of God (Acts 20:27), not just a short list of the usual evangelism passages.

2. **Church leaders should call members to cut back on worldly entertainment.** Let's talk screen time (computer, phone, and television). That's because for most of us, this competes greatly with time otherwise spent in prayer, meditating on the word of God, and sharing the good news with a lost world. With schedules packed with three to five hours daily of online leisure, no wonder we have little time for outreach, fellowship, and meeting the needs of those in pain. We must deal with our hearts (Proverbs 4:23).

3. **As for pornography, good shepherds assume nothing.** They call the entire church to sexual purity—probing gently, yet firmly calling for repentance.

4. **All leaders must model humility.** They must welcome feedback, rejecting the damaging clergy/laity (ministry/nonministry) system with its elitist terminology (Acts 20:19). Humility also means

seeking input from outside our local fellowship.

5. **Leaders must minister to the lost, not just the saved.** For the majority, this will probably mean heading up an evangelistic small group. They should seek those who have been driven away from the Lord through harsh, abusive leadership. They must also pursue those who have been caught up in sin or left the Lord because of doubts or lost of faith.

6. **The sheep are liable too.** Even though the Lord expects more of the shepherds—and rightly so—*all* of us are responsible to build ourselves up in the faith (Jude 20).

7. **All of us must be eager to help the poor** (Galatians 2:10). Historically, the church got into trouble when most of the money it collected went to pay for salaries and buildings. I am against neither; it's a matter of balance. Matthew 25 and Matthew 28 are complementary ministries.

Don't Rock the Boat?

Too many leaders aren't alarmed by their own sins or those of others. They fear challenging the sin of the church for the negative impact it might have on contribution. As one evangelist sheepishly stated, "We can't call people to the kind of biblical commitment that we use to, they won't stand for it." Church leaders do not feed and lead the flock, but tolerate widespread infidelity to God—more on this in the next chapter. Also alarming, some leaders think they have "arrived." They see no need for continued discipleship, input outside their congregation, or biblical education. Optimists inflate how well their churches are doing, while pessimists lack the imagination (and faith) to plot a new course and go forward. None of this needs to be the case. Repentance brings times of refreshing (Acts 3:19).

Here's another response from a newsletter reader:

> Thank you so much for unapologetically calling us to repent and reflect on the times of Ezekiel. In your articles you have urged us, "Don't be a silent or sideline critic. Speak up respectfully." But I don't think some of our leaders—and members—want to hear the truth, since they prefer the status quo.

Don't be a sideline critic *or* a passive leader. The Lord holds accountable shepherd and sheep alike. We can change. Let's not be people who fear rocking the boat.

Reflection:

Decisions:

5 Ezekiel Reprimands the False Prophets

This chapter focuses on the false prophets of Ezekiel 13. (For more on this, read Ezekiel 14–15 and 21.) As we will see, the problem is not so much false doctrines (like "circumcision is optional") as a lack of urgency coupled with stubborn refusal to confront sin. The prophets are misleading the Judeans through denying the seriousness of God's promises and warnings.

> The word of the LORD came to me: "Son of man, prophesy against the prophets of Israel who are now prophesying. Say to those who prophesy out of their own imagination: 'Hear the word of the LORD!' This is what the Sovereign LORD says: Woe to the foolish prophets who follow their own spirit and have seen nothing!" (13:1–3)

The prophecies do not represent God's thoughts. Their origin is psychological. For more on the dynamics of prophecy not rooted in the Word, see Jeremiah 23.

Notice, however, that Ezekiel does not deny that these are actual prophets, as this isn't the issue. There's a nice parallel in Matthew 7:22.

> "Your prophets, Israel, are like jackals among ruins. You have not gone up to the breaches in the wall to repair it for the people of Israel so

that it will stand firm in the battle on the day of the LORD. Their visions are false and their divinations a lie. Even though the LORD has not sent them, they say, 'The LORD declares,' and expect him to fulfill their words." (13:4–6)

Judah lies in ruins, spiritually speaking, although her physical desolation is also well underway. In Scripture, jackals are often seen scavenging among ruins (Jeremiah 9:11; also Isaiah 13:21–22; 34:13; Jeremiah 10:22; 49:33; 51:37; Lamentations 5:18). These prophets are active—walking amidst the ruins of God's people—yet they do nothing constructive.

These men are not building up God's people—who, like the modern church, are in a sorry state. We shall return to the matter of the breaches in the wall in Chapter 8, on Ezekiel 22.

They have convinced themselves, even as they attempt to convince others, that their feel-good message is divine in origin.

"Because they lead my people astray, saying, 'Peace,' when there is no peace, and because, when a flimsy wall is built, they cover it with whitewash, therefore tell those who cover it with whitewash that it is going to fall. Rain will come in torrents, and I will send hailstones hurtling down, and violent winds will burst forth. When the wall collapses, will people not ask you, 'Where is the whitewash you covered it with?'" (13:10–12)

The prophets make light of sin—exactly Jeremiah's complaint in Jeremiah 6:13–14. Jeremiah (active 626–586 BC) was the contemporary of Ezekiel (active in the 590s and 580s). The former prophesied mainly in Israel, the latter preaching in Babylon. (Ezekiel wasn't the only true prophet at this time!) For more on this, please review the *Jeremiah, Jesus & Us* series, accessible in my 2016 newsletters.[6]

The wall is flimsy to begin with, but they try to make it look safer by applying a coat of whitewash—because appearances are everything. How do modern "prophets" whitewash sin and faithlessness? Here are a few ways:

- **Lowering the standards of discipleship:** conversion without repentance, church membership without commitment or accountability to men or God.

- **Twisting Jesus' words "judge not"** (Matthew 7:1).[7] Instead of loving engagement, there's hands-off nonjudgmentalism—in sync with the world's notion that there is neither Judge nor judgment day.

- **Mirroring the postmodern emphasis on "journey" over destination.** Biblically, both are important—the way *as well as* coming to the Father (John 14:6).

- **Mirroring the world's rejection of "criticism" as "shaming."** In the world it is not cool to challenge people on their personal lifestyle, beliefs, behaviors, or faith. This has filtered into the church and is even espoused by Christian counselors.

- **Refusing to accept God's plan for family and sexuality**—instead caving in and leaving an impression of open-mindedness rather than biblical conviction.

- **Relying on past victories and gains**—in place of present commitment and faithfulness.

- **Giving a good sermon, yet looking the other way when God's words are ignored.** There is no real expectation of change—no follow-up, just cheap grace.

When false prophets and feckless leaders do not expose sin, collapse is inevitable.

"So I will pour out my wrath against the wall and against those who covered it with whitewash. I will say to you, 'The wall is gone and so are those who whitewashed it, those prophets of Israel who prophesied to Jerusalem and saw visions of peace for her when there was no peace, declares the Sovereign LORD'" (13:13–16).

These are Jeremiah's words in Lamentations 2:14 after the fall of Jerusalem:

> *The visions of your prophets*
> *   were false and worthless;*
> *they did not expose your sin*
> *   to ward off your captivity.*
> *The prophecies they gave you*
> *   were false and misleading.*

Ezekiel 13 continues with prophecies against sorcerers—women who practice the magic arts, who are also culpable of minimizing Judah's spiritual plight (13:17–23). These sorcerers prey on the anxious or gullible—people especially vulnerable to manipulation in times of crisis. Yet whereas the prophets' activity was public, the sorcerers' was private.

Popularity

Did the popular prophets utter falsehoods? Yes; they misrepresented Yahweh. The chief quality of their deluded prophecy was more than doctrinal error. It was the lie that the holy God doesn't really require repentance—that his people will be just fine coasting for a while. In our own day such prophets abound. How many sermons have you heard lately calling for radical repentance?

Last, for those of us who preach and teach, are we

taking our cues from the world, or are we digging deep into Scripture and holding forth God's word—regardless of how popular or unpopular this makes us?

Reflection:

Decisions:

6 · Ingratitude and Infidelity ·

Let's mentally transport ourselves back to the sixth century BC. The two chapters of Ezekiel we consider here are among the most graphic in all of Scripture. Both reveal an astounding degree of thanklessness toward Yahweh, as well as covenant infidelity. (Please read Ezekiel 16 and 23 in full before reading this chapter.) God's people today too owe a debt of gratitude. How *faithful* have we been to God?

> The word of the LORD came to me: "Son of man, confront Jerusalem with her detestable practices and say, 'This is what the Sovereign LORD says to Jerusalem: Your ancestry and birth were in the land of the Canaanites; your father was an Amorite and your mother a Hittite. On the day you were born your cord was not cut, nor were you washed with water to make you clean, nor were you rubbed with salt or wrapped in cloths. No one looked on you with pity or had compassion enough to do any of these things for you. Rather, you were thrown out into the open field, for on the day you were born you were despised'" (16:1–5).

The point is that Israel, intended to be a light among the nations, has ended up being no different from them—idolatrous and pagan. In a similar way, the modern church has lost its distinctiveness—its "salt" (Matthew 5:13).

His majesty and (above all) his holiness have been dishonored.

Yahweh provides a powerful illustration: his people as a helpless child, a discarded infant daughter—the sort of action for which the Canaanites were punished.

> *"'Then I passed by and saw you kicking about in your blood, and as you lay there in your blood I said to you, "Live!" I made you grow like a plant of the field. You grew and developed and entered puberty. Later I passed by, and when I looked at you and saw that you were old enough for love, I spread the corner of my garment over you and covered your naked body. I gave you my solemn oath and entered into a covenant with you, declares the Sovereign LORD, and you became mine'"* (16:6–8).

Yahweh protects and cares for his daughter. Under his care, she matures.

Eventually he marries her. Many books in the Bible picture a marriage relationship between God and his people—in the New Testament, the church is to be the bride of Christ (Ephesians 5:31–32; Revelation 19:7).

> *"'But you trusted in your beauty and used your fame to become a prostitute'"* (16:15).

Tragically, she trusted in her beauty, rather than appreciating and keeping her faith in God. In her pride she became arrogant.

She plunges into sin, becoming a prostitute. Yet this chapter isn't about sexual sin, but spiritual adultery. God's bride (Israel) was unfaithful to him (v.32; see James 4:4).

She has forgotten where she came from and who it was who loved her and took care of her (v.22; see 2 Peter 1:9).

There are many other sins mentioned in the chapters, for example, sacrificing her children—helpless newborns—to the Ammonite god Molech. (The children were incinerated.)

"'I am filled with fury against you, declares the Sovereign LORD, when you do all these things, acting like a brazen prostitute!'" (16:30)

Yahweh's wrath is richly earned. Jerusalem will be judged (v.38).

"'As surely as I live, declares the Sovereign LORD, your sister Sodom and her daughters never did what you and your daughters have done. Now this was the sin of your sister Sodom: She and her daughters were arrogant, overfed and unconcerned; they did not help the poor and needy. They were haughty and did detestable things before me. Therefore I did away with them as you have seen'" (16:48–50).

God's people have become like Sodom (Genesis 18).

Their sins include arrogance, overeating ("abundant food" NASB) at a time when there were plenty of poor people with whom they ought to have been sharing, "careless ease" (NASB), and failing to help poor and needy. Other detestable things are hinted at, presumably the notorious sexual perversion of Sodom and Gomorrah. Injustice, favoritism, judgmentalism, greed, harsh treatment of refugees, and sins of nationalism might be added to the list.

Yet these behaviors are merely symptomatic; the root sin is caring only about themselves. How like the modern West, where even for believers, life is all about the "managed pursuit of pleasure" (Miroslav Volf) instead of the pursuit of holiness. There is little discernible difference between the church and the world. As a bumper sticker sadly relates: "The only difference between Christians and sinners—Forgiveness."

> *This is what the Sovereign LORD says: "I will deal with you as you deserve, because you have despised my oath by breaking the covenant. Yet I will remember the covenant I made with you in the days of your youth, and I will establish an everlasting covenant with you" (16:59–60).*

Her sin is especially grievous because she knew better (Luke 12:47–48; John 12:47–48). She has broken the covenant.

Looking to an epoch far ahead, Yahweh foresees a time of eventual forgiveness (vs.60–63).

Are we that different from ancient Sodom?

As one mature brother in Christ put it, "I rarely if ever hear a sermon or a series of sermons on helping the poor. Ezekiel 16:49 is more relevant today than ever. From the outset of the liberation of God's people from Egyptian bondage, God's care for the weak—especially the widow, orphan, and alien—reverberates throughout the Old Testament (Leviticus 19:9–10, 15; 25:25–26; Deuteronomy 15:7–10; Psalms 82:3–4; 140:12; Proverbs 14:21, 31; 17:5; 19:17; 21:13; 22:22–23; 29:7; Isaiah 58:6–10; 61:1). The New Testament further confirms that this is God's heart (James 1:27; Matthew 5:3; 11:5; 19:21; 25:31–46; Acts 9:36; 10:2; Romans 15:26; 2 Corinthians 9:9; Galatians 2:10). We are not living out God's heart in caring for our own community of believers, let alone the non-Christian community around us.

Oholah and Oholibah

In chapter 23 Yahweh continues to shake his people awake, again using sexual metaphor to spotlight the need for covenant fidelity.

> *The word of the LORD came to me: "Son of man, there were two women, daughters of the same mother. They became prostitutes in Egypt, engaging in prostitution from their youth. In that land their breasts were fondled and their virgin bosoms caressed. The older was named Oholah, and her sister was Oholibah. They were mine and gave birth to sons and daughters. Oholah is Samaria, and Oholibah is Jerusalem" (23:1–4).*

Here Israel (its capital city of Samaria having been destroyed by the Assyrians) and Judah (its capital city of Jerusalem being devastated by the Babylonians) are compared to two immoral sisters.

Just as judgment fell on northern Israel (eighth

century BC), so it would come upon southern Judah (sixth century).

Ezekiel 23 has been described as the message of Hosea in a parable. The rest of the chapter will shock those unfamiliar with the Old Testament, as it will those who do not realize the seriousness of a covenant. (I remember being taken aback by Ezekiel 16 and 23 when I first read them—and they are still hard to read.) Although we do not have time in this chapter to explore the entire chapter, I hope you will do a serious read of Ezekiel 23.

The revolting imagery—even more graphic than chapter 16—was absolutely necessary. So far have God's people drifted from him that a shock is needed. This is their last chance to repent before the approaching Babylonian doom.

God's people are trusting in political power, treaties, coercion, and military might. Ironically, they will soon be destroyed by the very nations to which they have turned for security (23:22–25).

The Bible is not vague when it comes to identifying sin. Sins detailed in chapter 23 include: idolatry (v.7), adultery (v.37), Sabbath breaking (v.38), infant sacrifice (v.39), desecrating the sanctuary, and dishonoring Yahweh (v.38).

Questions for the Modern Church

The words of Ezekiel aren't outdated. The vast majority of churchgoers today have been equally unfaithful, equally ungrateful. Sex and violence—there is plenty of both in Ezekiel 16 and 23—may have been the only things that would get his people's attention. (How similar our culture is!) Please take a moment to consider how the message applies to you and to us as a church.

- What does it take to get my attention?

- Am I disengaged from the mission of the church?

- Have my relationships in the body of Christ become shallow and ineffectual?

- Am I faithful to my covenant promises (made in my baptismal pledge)?

- Is Jesus still Lord—*really* Lord?

- Am I grateful?

- As a church, have we become like Sodom? Do we spend more time focused on the pursuit of leisure and entertainment, or on the pursuit of holiness? Are we heedless of others' needs?

- Christian leaders, are we alarmed by the nonchalant worldliness of the church?

- Do we have the courage to address sin—and follow up? (Mere words are not enough.)

- Do we believe in the necessity of actual obedience?

Reflection:

Decisions:

7   • The Lord Is Just •

At some point or another, most of us have bristled at some of the harder teachings of Scripture, perhaps wondering whether the Lord was being arbitrary or unfair. After all, there are many judgment passages in the Bible, and the majority of people do not repent. Surely the Lord doesn't prefer it this way! For this reason, as a young Christian I was strengthened by Ezekiel 18. The final verse reads: "For I take no pleasure in the death of anyone, declares the Sovereign Lord. Repent and live!" (If you're a young believer, *please* take a moment to read the entire chapter.)

Scripture assures us that God is good. Yet in our limited perspective (we are familiar with only the smallest sliver of time and eternity) and basing our opinions on our own feelings and individualistic standards, not God's, we misinterpret the Lord's righteous acts and judgments.

How about this book so far? Too direct? Not enough grace? Or was Ezekiel himself too harsh—expecting too much commitment? Is the Lord perhaps unfair to call us to holiness? This was a frequent complaint of the Israelites throughout their history. (For example, see Numbers 16!) As we will read, God is by no means unfair.

A Proverb

Ezekiel 18 begins with a proverb. Proverbs appear not

only in the Book of Proverbs; they're scattered through Scripture. Only a fraction of the old Jewish proverbs were written down in the Bible; for example, Solomon spoke 3000 (1 Kings 4:32). Ezekiel 18:2 was a popular (nonbiblical) proverb—one rejected by the Lord. (It also shows up in Jeremiah 31:29.)

> *The word of the LORD came to me: "What do you people mean by quoting this proverb about the land of Israel:*
> *'The parents eat sour grapes,*
> *and the children's teeth are set on edge'?*
> *"As surely as I live, declares the Sovereign LORD, you will no longer quote this proverb in Israel. For everyone belongs to me, the parent as well as the child—both alike belong to me. The one who sins is the one who will die"* (18:1–4).

The adage suggests that the current woes of God's people stem from the previous generation. That would mean Judah isn't being treated fairly; they aren't personally responsible for the current spiritual malaise. (See also Lamentations 5:7.) But this is wrong! The present generation is extremely sinful! The specific sins listed in this chapter provide a window into the profound moral failings of God's people.

> *"The one who sins is the one who will die. The child will not share the guilt of the parent, nor will the parent share the guilt of the child. The*

righteousness of the righteous will be credited to them, and the wickedness of the wicked will be charged against them" (18:20).

The Lord insists that he is just in rewarding or punishing his people.

This verse obviously contradicts the doctrine of original sin (c. AD 400), the notion that humans are born damned, having inherited Adam's sin and guilt. Yahweh is just!

> *"But if a wicked person turns away from all the sins they have committed and keeps all my decrees and does what is just and right, that person will surely live; they will not die. None of the offenses they have committed will be remembered against them. Because of the righteous things they have done, they will live. Do I take any pleasure in the death of the wicked? declares the Sovereign LORD. Rather, am I not pleased when they turn from their ways and live? But if a righteous person turns from their righteousness and commits sin and does the same detestable things the wicked person does, will they live? None of the righteous things that person has done will be remembered. Because of the unfaithfulness they are guilty of and because of the sins they have committed, they will die"* (18:21–24).

God is not only fair; he is also responsive to our hearts. When we pull away, he distances himself from us (allows punishment). When we draw near to him, he draws near to us, gladly offering a clean slate and a fresh start.

Yahweh takes no pleasure in punishment, judgment, or death.

> *"Yet you say, 'The way of the LORD is not just.' Hear, you Israelites: Is my way unjust? Is it not your ways that are unjust? If a righteous person turns from their righteousness and commits sin, they will die for it; because of the sin they have committed they will die. But if a wicked person turns away from the wickedness they have committed and does what is just and right, they will save their life. Because they consider all the offenses they have committed and turn away from them, that person will surely live; they will not die. Yet the Israelites say, 'The way of the LORD is not just.' Are my ways unjust, people of Israel? Is it not your ways that are unjust?"* (18:25–29)

The Israelites have it exactly backwards. *They* are the ones who are unjust (not living righteously), not Yahweh. They seem unwilling to take an honest look in the mirror and to accept the truth about their lives.

Although this chapter is limited to Ezekiel 18, we easily discern God's justice in many other chapters, like 25–32 and 35, where truth is declared to the countries neighboring Israel. The Lord has forgotten no one; every good deed will be rewarded, every evil deed will be punished, no one will slip through the cracks, and everything will be just. (Not necessarily in this world—but ultimately, at the day of reckoning.)

> *"Therefore, you Israelites, I will judge each of you according to your own ways, declares the Sovereign LORD. Repent! Turn away from all your offenses; then sin will not be your downfall. Rid yourselves of all the offenses you have committed, and get a new heart and a new spirit. Why will you die, people of Israel? For I take no pleasure in the death of anyone, declares the Sovereign LORD. Repent and live!"* (18:30–32)

Lives can change—not on our own, but with the Lord's help (36:26). He offers a new heart and a new start. Thus we see that the Lord is not only just, but also generous.

These Judeans have *not* been unfairly treated. Through the prophetic warnings and even through waves of exile, Yahweh has sought to get their attention in hopes they will repent. For instead of standing apart from the world—and worldly religion—God's people have blended in, adopting pagan practices and abandoning holiness. And they have rationalized it all! (See Ephesians 4:17–19; Romans 1:20–23.)

How like modern Christianity this is! We have not only drifted form God's righteous standards, but also lost our ability to *hear* his words. We have an excuse for everything. Jesus cried, "He who has an ear to ear, let him hear" (Revelation 3:22). As individuals or even as churches, we must ask ourselves: "Am I (are we) earless?"

In such challenging conditions, what does God expect *me* to do? We will try to answer that question in the next chapter.

Reflection:

Decisions:

8   • Stand in the Gap! •

As has been emphasized repeatedly in this book, there are numerous parallels between sixth century BC Judah and the Christian church of the twenty-first century Although there are bright areas and positive developments here and there, overall the major trends are downward.

- **We seem to have lost our mission.**[8] As a friend of mine in another faith tradition observed about my own fellowship: "It's going to be hard to grow with a mission you no longer believe in." Few talk about winning the world for Christ, and fewer still about planting new churches. No wonder the majority of congregations are shrinking or seeing only marginal growth.

- **Sin is only lightly addressed, whether publicly or privately.** There is a widespread lack of conviction about holiness. Holiness is a major theme in Ezekiel. It dominates chapters 40–48. In many ways, the theology of Ezekiel is that of Leviticus: "Be holy, because I the Lord your God am holy" (Leviticus 19:2).

- **We care little for those in need**—though, as it

was in Ezekiel's day, we care plenty about ourselves (16:48–49).

- **Materialism is a huge issue.** Many Christians seem to be trying to make as much money as Christianly possible. Paul warned us about those who are "lovers of themselves [and] lovers of money" (2 Timothy 3:2).

- **People are confused about salvation,** more than happy to lower the bar of repentance and dispense with biblical baptism. Have we become so "tolerant" that we don't really believe the world is lost? (1 John 5:19).

- **Churches track with the world on controversial issues** (sexuality, ethics, "diversity" without acceptance, politics, etc.). We don't like taking strong moral stands.

- **The word of God is no longer respected** (as in our postmodern world, truth has become relative). Systematic biblical teaching is optional or ignored.

- **Courageous leadership is in short supply.** Many talk about past victories rather than facing the present with realism, courage, and faith.

Despite all this, there is still an arrogant spirit toward outsiders—an unwillingness to learn from others who are making an impact for God and encouraging genuine biblical faith. It is simply not enough to rely on occasional doctrinal or practical adjustments. We need fresh eyes. Let's invite believers from godly churches to share what they observe about our fellowship. When we're self-assured (and numb to reality), like ancient Israel, we are neither wise nor godly.

Taking a Stand

Ezekiel Chapter 22 is a call to action. If we are outnumbered by those who should be supporting us as our spiritual brothers and sisters—yet who resist the biblical message—will we stand up and be counted?

> The word of the LORD came to me: "Son of man, will you judge her? Will you judge this city of bloodshed? Then confront her with all her detestable practices... Son of man, say to the land, 'You are a land that has not been cleansed or rained on in the day of wrath'" (22:1–2, 24).

The charges in this chapter read like "a catalogue of crime" (Peter C. Craigie, "Ezekiel," in the *Daily Study Bible*). Jerusalem is a sinful city, and her judgment is certain. Moral behavior flows from healthy faith, yet in her case what flows are bloodshed, idolatry, oppressing aliens, wronging the fatherless and widows, Sabbath violation, various sexual sins, bribery, poor workplace ethics, and unholiness.

Princes, Priests, Prophets and the People

Although the people are culpable, the leaders are held most accountable—as is usually the case throughout God's word.

> *"Her priests do violence to my law and profane my holy things... they shut their eyes to the keeping of my Sabbaths... Her officials within her are like wolves tearing their prey... [for] unjust gain... Her prophets whitewash these deeds for them by false visions... The people of the land practice extortion and commit robbery; they oppress the poor and needy and mistreat the foreigner, denying them justice"* (22:26–29).

Leaders' lives are selfishly directed. Religious leaders (prophets and priests) minimize the severity of the situation. Political leaders (princes and officials) are no better.

Likewise, those *not* in prominent positions of influence are self-centered too. Nor are they alarmed about Israel's sorry spiritual state.

Yet acting as if things are fine does not change the reality. The Titanic is still sinking.

> *"I looked for someone among them who would build up the wall and stand before me in the gap on behalf of the land so I would not have to destroy it, but I found no one. So I will pour out my wrath on them and consume them with my fiery anger, bringing down on their own heads all they have done, declares the Sovereign LORD"* (22:30–31).

As with ancient Sodom (Genesis 18:20), judgment is near—and richly deserved.

Yahweh seeks even *one* person to "stand in the gap." Am I that person? If yes, am I standing up and being counted, taking a stand? If not, why not?

Perspective and Challenge

Ezekiel wasn't claiming there were *no* righteous people. Ezekiel, after all, would be an obvious exception. We are reminded of Yahweh's words through Jeremiah:

> "Go up and down the streets of Jerusalem,
>   look around and consider,
>   search through her squares.
> If you can find but one person
>   who deals honestly and seeks the truth,
>   I will forgive this city" (Jeremiah 5:1).

Jeremiah and his faithful disciple Baruch were certainly faithful to God. Scripture often utilizes hyperbole to make a point. Yet this qualification hardly softens the situation. The Lord intends us to take seriously the call to rise up, stand in the gap, and repair the wall wherever there is a breach. This is personal: If I am not going to stand up and be counted, who is? Vital areas include:

- Involvement in the body of Christ (Colossians 1:28–2:1)
- Insisting on a close relationship with the Lord (Colossians 2:6–7)
- Investing in knowing God's word (Colossians 3:16)
- Sharing my faith (Colossians 4:5–6)

Let us not give in to despair. Yet neither let us conform, rationalize, or shrink back from the call to action.

Reflection:

Decisions:

Reflection:

9   •   A Beautiful Singer? •

Ezekiel preaches for many years, warning his compatriots that Yahweh means business when he calls for repentance and holiness. By the time we reach chapter 33, Jerusalem has already fallen. Ezekiel's prediction has come to pass; the prophet has been vindicated. He is now something of a celebrity.

Yet some are still optimistic, holding on to a vain hope. They reason, "Abraham was promised the land, and he was only one person—whereas we are many! Surely Israel is still ours—this is only a temporary setback." This is their reasoning (33:24), despite the fact that Jerusalem lies in ruins!

While the poorer Jews remain in the land of Israel, the cream of Judah is now in exile. They are the ones who applaud Ezekiel—and who appear now to even *enjoy* his messages!

> *"As for you, son of man, your people are talking together about you by the walls and at the doors of the houses, saying to each other, 'Come and hear the message that has come from the LORD.' My people come to you, as they usually do, and sit before you to hear your words, but they do not put them into practice. Their mouths speak of love, but their hearts are greedy for unjust gain. Indeed, to them you are nothing more than one who sings love songs with a beautiful voice and plays an instrument well, for they hear your words but do not put them into practice. When all this*

comes true—and it surely will—then they will know that a prophet has been among them" (33:30–33).

Ezekiel now enjoys a solid reputation. They really like his preaching—but for his style and delivery, or for its content?

Acclaim and audience size do not necessarily mean the audience is *listening*. Despite their approbation, the people's hearts are in the wrong place. Like Simon Magus (Acts 8:23), they are full of greed. They have become inured to the Word. They hear it, but it does not penetrate. These people have no intention to hold themselves—let alone others—accountable to the demands of God's word.

Despite their superficially positive attitude, they are disobedient to God. There *will* be accountability—to the Lord.

Why I'm Concerned

As in Ezekiel's time, today there are many popular speakers. The evangelical world is full of *megachurches,* with *megapersonalities* who draw *megacrowds.* Sometimes the speaker has diluted the word of God—refusing to take a biblical stand, instead offering saccharine substitutes for God's word. Even among the family of churches I belong to, the word is preached, and the crowd applauds, but there is no lasting effect: no repentance, no godly enthusiasm, no alarm, no commitment to change.

Far too many congregations take their cue from the "successful." If this is the direction in which we're headed—if we are uncritically following these broader trends—I am deeply concerned.

Often modern "church" reminds me of Ezekiel 33. Here's why—there are a few things we may observe:

- **Performer-spectator mentality.** People expect a show. Those who go up on stage before the congregation may even be referred to as "entertainers" or "performers." The audience rates church on the quality of the performance and whether their children were entertained. Applause is given, and some speakers expect it.

- **Consumer Christianity.** People select a church based on the services provided, rather than on whether the Word is being preached and the congregation is in the habit of obeying the message.

- **Inflated reputations.** Jesus points out that some churches have reputations for being alive, yet they are dead—asleep (Revelation 3:1). Further, just because a church is widely recommended doesn't mean it's on track biblically.

- **Celebrity speakers.** Guest preachers or conference speakers are typically those with *personality* (what about character?), *storytelling ability* (what about feeding God's people from the Word?), or *confidence* (ego). Do we distinguish Diotrephes from Demetrius (3 John 9, 12)? For that matter, do we invite those who will challenge our traditions—"outsiders"—or only "insiders"? Is it the same speakers year after year? We measure ourselves, by ourselves.

- **Materialism.** *Selfish gain* was the real agenda for Ezekiel's listeners, and Mammon is alive and well today. Christians' lifestyles are seldom distinguishable from those of their neighbors—same attitudes and habits vis-à-vis spending, savings, prestige buying, fashion, sports, recreation, entertainment, politics, etc. Recall Yahweh's constant challenge to Israel (16:48).

A Final Thought

Ezekiel 33 is a powerful passage. As we have seen, it takes little effort to apply it to our own situation. So let us keep this in mind: *Religious* doesn't mean *righteous*. And *attendance* isn't *attentiveness*.

Reflection:

Decisions:

10 • Glorious Future •

What future? Weren't Ezekiel's words primarily "doom and gloom"? Isn't it too late for the people of Judah—and for us? Despite the hard words, Yahweh isn't finished with Israel. A remnant will return to the land (538 BC). And centuries later, some Jews—faithful and obedient—will be awaiting the messianic kingdom.

God does not change. His glory remains undiminished, and his purposes firm. But then as now, *holiness* is the order of the day.

> *"I will give you a new heart and put a new spirit in you; I will remove from you your heart of stone and give you a heart of flesh"* (36:26).

Several times in Ezekiel the Lord says he will give his people a new heart. See chapters 26, 36, and 39.

While there are a few bright spots in the history of God's people from Ezekiel's time onward, this promise is more directly fulfilled in New Testament times, with the outpouring of the Spirit (Acts 2:33).

> *This is what the Sovereign LORD says: "My people, I am going to open your graves and bring you up from them; I will bring you back to the land of Israel"* (37:12).

There are hints here of the general resurrection—the time when the dead will be raised following the Lord's return, before the judgment day. But that isn't the import of the passage. The return of Israel to its land (which happened in 538 BC) is pictured as a sort of national resurrection. A fresh, new beginning is within reach.

> *I saw the glory of the God of Israel coming from the east. His voice was like the roar of rushing waters, and the land was radiant with his glory. The vision I saw was like the vision I had seen when he came to destroy the city and like the visions I had seen by the Kebar River, and I fell facedown. The glory of the LORD entered the temple through the gate facing east. Then the Spirit lifted me up and brought me into the inner court, and the glory of the LORD filled the temple (43:2–5).*

There is a new Promised Land and a new temple. (*Note:* the images fail if taken literally—they make far better geographical, historical, and theological sense when understood symbolically.)

Yahweh's *shekhinah,* the glory of his presence, fills the temple just as it did at the end of Exodus (with the completion of the Tabernacle) and at the dedication of Solomon's temple.

Ezekiel's New Jerusalem even has 12 gates (48:21), like the New Jerusalem of Revelation 21:21. Again, none of these amazing images are fulfilled in Old Testament times—nor even in the first century or in the early church

(AD 30–325). Complete fulfillment will not take place this side of the Lord's return.

Yahweh-shammah

The last two words of Ezekiel are the name of the holy city, the New Jerusalem. They are *Yahweh-shammah*.

> "And the name of the city from that time on will be: the LORD is there" (48:35).

It's all about relationship—not architecture. If we want this relationship, we must live holy lives (Hebrews 12:14). For more on why this is indispensable, check out the article in this note at the end of the book.[9]

We are in fact *more* responsible than the Jews of Ezekiel's day (Hebrews 10:26–31).

Perspective

Biblical scholar John Taylor put it well:

> For Ezekiel, the climax has been reached: but it was still only a vision. John, the exile in Patmos, who saw Ezekiel's words fulfilled in the coming of Christ as Emmanuel, God with us, also looked forward to the day when a great voice would be heard from the throne saying, 'Behold, the dwelling of God is with men. He will dwell with them, and they shall be his people' (Rev 21:3). The glory of heaven is the ultimate fulfillment of all. It is to that great culmination that all Ezekiel's readers should be led.[10]

So how should we feel about Ezekiel's message (and this little book)? What does this mean for the modern church?

- **We can be encouraged.** The truth—no matter how hard—will set us free.

- **Ultimately, it's not all about church.** Regardless of the level of apathy—or energy—of the modern church, we are called to live faithful lives. We will be let down by fellow believers, even as we let others down. Like Peter, we should avoid asking, "Lord, what about him?" (John 21:21).

- **Nor is the "bottom line" numerical** (attendance, baptisms, donations). The Lord examines the heart. He is not fooled by clever statistics.

Reflection:

Decisions:

• Conclusion •

Ezekiel was a powerful prophet. Yahweh gave him a devastatingly strong message, affording his people an opportunity to repent while there was still time on the clock.

I know that many were challenged by this series as it appeared in the newsletter, beginning with the earliest installments. But since then, *what have we actually changed?* Has there been repentance, or do we feel so secure that we haven't made any changes at all? Are we more evangelistic now? More prayerful? If we're leaders, have we determined to lay out the whole counsel of God, without apology? After preaching or teaching, do we hope for "positive feedback" more than for change?

And if this was your first time to read Ezekiel, please commit to more serious study. God speaks in *every* book within Scripture; every one of them is God-breathed and useful (2 Timothy 3:16–17).

What is my responsibility?

We aren't responsible for others' responses, but for our own. We shouldn't necessarily blame ourselves if an outsider doesn't show up for a Christian event, or an insider decides to walk away from the Lord. But we are accountable to the Lord for our response to what he has revealed in his word. Am I listening? Am I critiquing the messenger, or examining the message?

For me, writing the Ezekiel series has been both eye-opening and personally challenging. Yet while I still have a distance to go in evangelism and prayer, I think I'm on a better track now. Of course, as long as we're in this world, we will not attain perfection. However, we *can* and *must* live a holy life (Hebrews 12:14).

Let's live for Christ. Let's show this sorry world who God is—and what real faith looks like. The future *will* be glorious if we repent and walk by faith. Yet the modern church—like ancient Israel—should be sobered by Jesus' ominous question:

"When the Son of Man comes, will he find faith on earth?" (Luke 18:8).

• Appendix •

Responses to the Ezekiel Series

Most of the following comments came from mature Christians—though the age range is from 20 to 90. These include elders, teachers, missionaries, evangelists, administrators, women's ministry leaders, and biblical scholars. Comments have come from every continent, and they have been overwhelmingly positive. I have edited some for brevity and clarity.

- "These posts have been excellent, focusing and helpful. They are not angry, mean or harsh. No finger pointing. A flashlight shone on the kitchen pests and a rock-solid call to love and obey the Lord."

- "Wow! the similarities between the two eras (then and now) is scary. We trust in guns more than God, and love the pursuit of happiness at any cost. We are well fed, arrogant, not caring for the poor, marinated in a hypersexualized culture. Lord help us!... Thank you so much for sounding the needed alarm, handling God's teachings with integrity, and not shying away from the inconvenient truth. We need to wake up. Our generation and the future need teaching like this regularly—before it's too late."

- "We are discussing these lessons in our church, especially among the men and the leaders. We need to return to biblical roots and motivation for making this about Jesus and his mission. If we *don't* rock the boat, we won't find out who is willing to walk on water. I am really focusing on being a person whose love for Father is seen in how I obey what he tells me to do (i.e. get out of the boat)... not on how much I talk about it. 'It is not what I preach, but what I tolerate' (quote from *Extreme Ownership*) in myself and others that displays love in God's terms."

- "Thank you for voicing many of my own feelings and concerns."

- "I appreciate your candor and boldness. This is a tremendous upward call and encouragement to live the holy life to which we have been called."

- "Keep preaching the truth and be a prophet. Our church is failing, and I am fearful of the consequences."

- "Thanks for your reflection on Ezekiel. It is to the point and well written."

- "I feel convicted in my own life but also inspired to bring this message back to those I lead in order to cultivate a deeper love of God and the Word in their lives."

- "What a timely, insightful, truth-filled, challenging, eye-opening, and serious warning to us all."

- "Thanks for the strong messages. I, and others, need them."

- "I recently prayed that God will show our fellowship its blind spots. Don't get me wrong; I do not want to blame our leaders or my church. I love the church and am involved in our women's leadership group. I just have the feeling the Spirit wants to show me something—I do not want to stop."

- "I found your article indicting, challenging—a breath of fresh air in a sea of excuses and dullness. Thank you for saying, 'The emperor has no clothes.' Hopefully this will stir some, especially in leadership, to face reality and take their heads out of the sand."

- "Thank you for the sobering assessment."

- "Tonight at our midweek meeting I read part of your piece out loud, and a great discussion followed. We heard your indictment of the modern church, going through each of the four lame excuses that block so many in our circles from hearing the message and taking it to heart. Everyone also appreciated the part about modern Christians, like the Jews, mistakenly thinking that they had received an irrevocable promise from the Lord regarding possession of the kingdom of God."

- "Here in Europe many brothers and sisters are talking about the series in a positive way. They are saying, in effect, 'Let's listen to this voice, and take stock of our hearts and churches.'"

- "I'm deeply concerned at how the general luke-warmness of the evangelical world has crept into our fellowship. This influences us more than does the Bible. I remember when we were counter-cultural, priding ourselves on being Bible-only Christians. I know that we all need to learn from other groups, but some have accepted mainstream Christianity as the standard—making us feel pretty good about *our* version. Strong, thoughtful prophetic preaching is needed to stir people out of comfortable lifestyles."

- "Leaders usually think I'm *exaggerating* the sorry state our congregations. I am observing similar reactions to your Ezekiel articles—no urgency for change. Their reasoning: Since this topic has been talked about for a while now, but no one has found a solution, it shouldn't be brought up again. In the past, we got shut down by leaders using authority over us. Today it happens in a nicer way—with a smile and by simply ignoring us... It is my opinion that we are looking for one big solution to a complex problem... There are many, many, many small things that we are doing / not doing that hurt our spiritual growth."

- "While there are many leaders who tacitly agree with the need to do more, a return to seeking true intimacy with God does not seem to be in the cards... Members are not taught or encouraged to practice the spiritual disciplines. It's always 'Bible study and prayer.' What happened to scripture memory? What happened to meditation, silence, solitude, simplicity, generosity, and submission? We are asking people to replicate what Jesus did during his three years of ministry, failing to realize that it took the Son of God decades of practicing the spiritual disciplines to be prepared to start his ministry... We are truly at a crossroads... "

- "Ezekiel is one of my favorite books. It is unique in its vision of God's throne (cherubim, wheels, and glory), the many special calls to repentance, and the hope expressed later in the book. What an awesome and neglected book—and perfect for our time. The call to action and repentance is encouraging and helpful. We accept it wholeheartedly."

- "I have thoroughly enjoyed your series on Ezekiel, and have benefited greatly from it. Thank you for being so sensitive, perceptive, and honest about the current state of the church and the desperate need for faithful obedience to Yahweh. In my eighty-seven years, I have served as a preaching minister, missionary, and elder during sixty-four of those years. My experience in ministry has verified the stark truth of what you have written in your articles based on Ezekiel's prophecy calling for renewal and recommitment to God and his self-revelation through his Son, Jesus the Christ. Thank you for casting a tall shadow of influence that is falling with healing power across the people of God all over the world."

- "Awesome and spot on. Your wife's insight [message 3] sliced through my heart. We must always remain on guard and call others to obedience of Scripture, imitating Jesus' life. We are too comfortable with the world..."

- "You have challenged me to my core. I sometimes wonder whether or not there's simply an unspoken agreement between leaders and followers to not touch the proverbial 'third rail' of American comfort and materialism—because we all just enjoy it way too much. I also appreciate your direct condemnation of too much 'screen time.' Passive entertainment is Satan's greatest tool to keep me from living a truly meaningful, fulfilling and effective Christ-centered life. Another direct hit! Thank you for issuing the clarion call for me to wake up and take action."

- "There's no doubt in my mind that we have allowed our culture to influence God's church in an ungodly manner. Many times it's hard to even see a distinction from the religious world that we live in (particularly here in America). Worldliness is Satan's greatest tool and deception that we face daily... There are too many souls at stake (including my own) to ignore what God has commanded us to be."

- "I deeply appreciate your love for God and his church, which you have demonstrated through the years by unflinchingly preaching and teaching the truths from God's word... I'm grateful for the clarion call to repentance... Once your series is complete, we plan to preach a series of sermons on Ezekiel for our own congregation. You are loved, respected and deeply appreciated by many, many of us around the globe... "

- "I think it would be alarming to many leaders to hear how many members supplement their spiritual growth by going out and listening to 'pastors' outside our fellowship. My experience is that this is almost the norm."

- "I once read with disbelief how a nation so blessed as Israel could turn away from the living God; however, as I get older I am not so quick to cast such judgements on Israel when I find our fellowship in not too different a place."

• Notes •

1. Lifeway Research, cited in Christianity Today, Sept 2019: 18.

2. https://www.douglasjacoby.com/newsletters/.

3. https://www.douglasjacoby.com/statistics-and-church-growth/.

4. Church history does not support the common practice of a church led by one man. Nor is there a single mention of evangelists as church leaders in any of the early Christian literature. If Timothy was the church leader in Ephesus, such a practice appears to be the exception, not the rule.

5. https://www.hopeandfreedom.com/clergy-sex-addiction-intensive.

6. https://www.douglasjacoby.com/newsletters/.

7. Please take a look at the study "Judge Not!" at https://www.douglasjacoby.com/judge-not/.

8. Here's a useful article: "Writing on the Wall—The Church Is Not Growing," https://churchleaders.com/outreach-missions/outreach-missions-articles/343247-church-not-growing.html.

9. Graydon Stephenson, "Holiness: 'Even the tassels are holy,'" https://www.douglasjacoby.com/holiness-even-tassels-holy-graydon-stephenson/.

10. John B. Taylor, in the *Tyndale Old Testament Commentaries*. Craigie's perspective is valuable too.

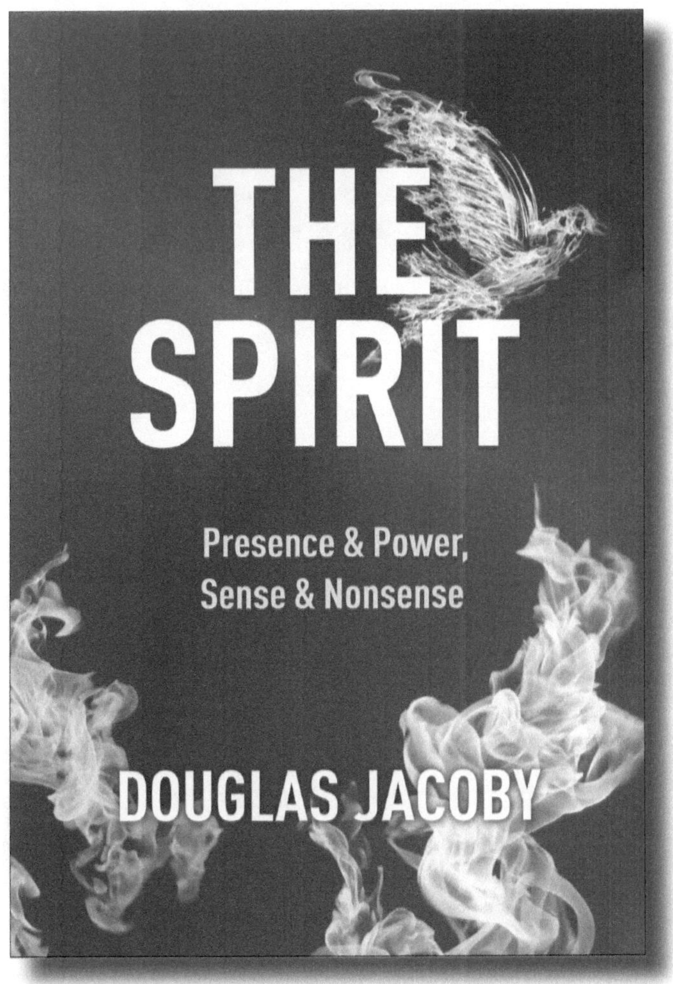
THE
SPIRIT
Presence & Power,
Sense & Nonsense
DOUGLAS JACOBY

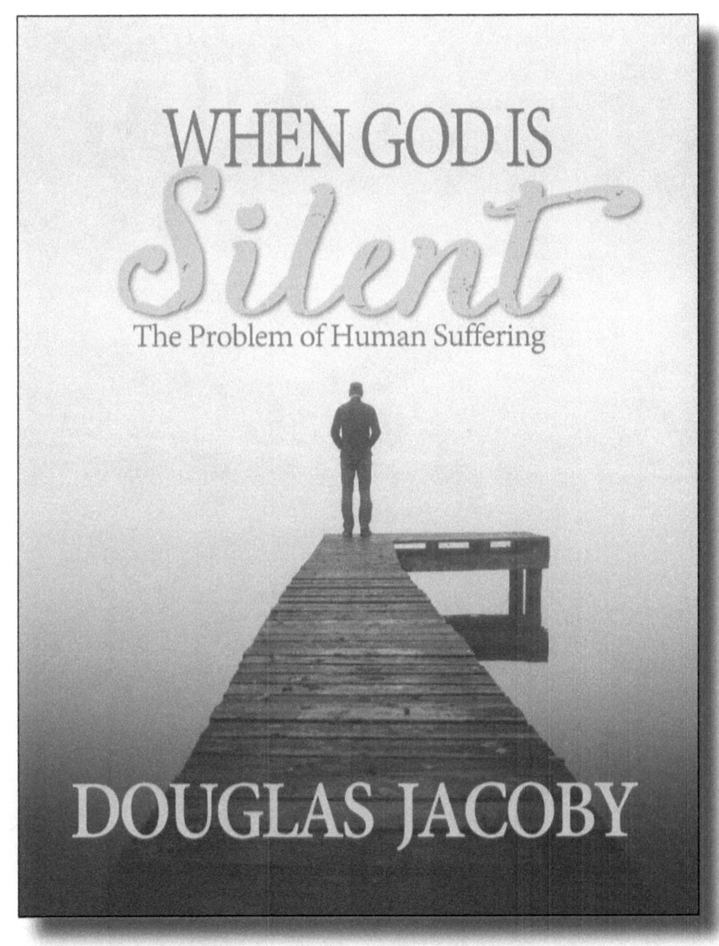
WHEN GOD IS
Silent
The Problem of Human Suffering
DOUGLAS JACOBY

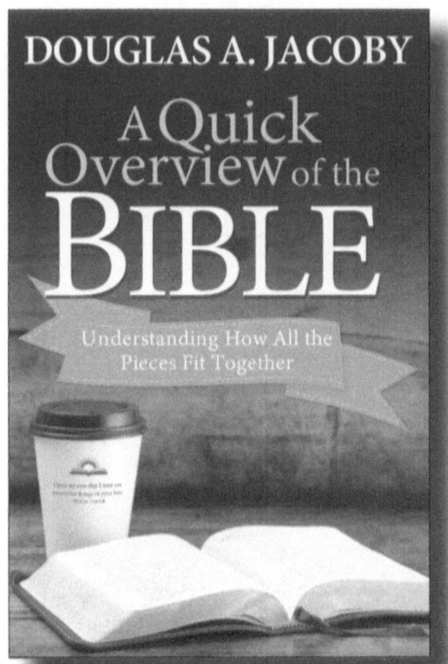
DOUGLAS A. JACOBY
A Quick
Overview of the
BIBLE
Understanding How All the
Pieces Fit Together

An Evangelism Handbook
for the 21st Century
Till the
NETS
Are Full
DOUGLAS JACOBY

Dr. Douglas Jacoby
EXODUS
Night of
Redemption

The Radical Life of Elijah
Chariots
of Fire
Dr. Douglas Jacoby

www.ipibooks.com